Nine O'Clock Lullaby

by Marilyn Singer

illustrated by Frané Lessac

HarperCollins*Publishers*

To those promising world travelers,
Sara and Amy Livingston

Acknowledgments

Many thanks to:
Steven Aronson
Renée Cafiero
Carlos Carvajal
Lynda Cassanos
Richard Choy
Martin Dooley
Liz Gordon
and, most especially, Leslie Kimmelman

M.S.

For Cody

F.L.

9 P.M. in Brooklyn, New York
The vroom and shush of traffic
outside the bedroom window
while Mama turns the pages
of a sleepytime tale.
9 P.M. in Brooklyn, New York, is…

10 P.M. in Puerto Rico

Sweet rice, fruit ice, coconut candy.

Papa playing congas, Tío his guitar.

Swaying lanterns in the branches,

dancing people on the grass.

Bedtime is forgotten on a special party night.

10 P.M. in Puerto Rico is…

Midnight on the mid-Atlantic
Nothing blacker than the water,
nothing wider than the sky.
Pitch and toss, pitch and toss.
The Big Dipper might just ladle
a drink out of the sea.
Midnight on the mid-Atlantic is…

2 A.M. in England
Bread in the pantry at nighttime
tastes better than cream cakes at tea.
2 A.M. in England is…

3 A.M. in Zaire
Dreaming by the Congo.

3 A.M. in Switzerland

Dreaming in the Alps.

3 A.M. in Zaire and Switzerland is…

5 A.M. in Moscow

A crash and a clatter
and the samovar on the floor.
The cat has done it again!
Papa wakes up with a laugh.
Mama wakes up with a shout.
Babushka doesn't wake at all,
but just stays snoring in her bed.
5 A.M. in Moscow, Russia, is…

7:30 A.M. in India
All over the village
well ropes squeak,
buckets splash,
bracelets jingle,
long braids swish.
All over the village
morning music.
7:30 A.M. in India is…

10 A.M. in Guangzhou, China
On the way to Goat City
auntie pedals quickly,
flying like a dragon.
On the way to Goat City
elder sister pedals slowly,
flapping like a goose.
10 A.M. in Guangzhou, China, is…

11 A.M. in Japan
In the pond
   grandfather floats a tulip
      so the fish can greet the spring.
11 A.M. in Japan is…

Noon in Sydney, Australia

At the barbie, five cousins, four uncles, three aunts,
two sheepdogs, six lizards, and one sly kookaburra
stealing sausage right off the plates.
Noon in Sydney, Australia, is…

3 P.M. in Samoa

The rain has stopped.

The sea is calm.

"Let's weave," say the mothers.

"Let's fish," say the fathers.

"Let's chase the dogs," say the brothers,

"before it rains again."

3 P.M. in Samoa is…

5 P.M. in Nome, Alaska

Toss the blanket high.

Toss the blanket higher.

Ask her, can she see the caribou?

Ask her, can she touch the sky?

5 P.M. in Nome, Alaska, is...

6 P.M. in Los Angeles
The sun eases down
like a big golden dinner plate
at the end of the day
on the beach.
6 P.M. in Los Angeles is...

8 P.M. in Mexico

Saying good night to the burros

8 P.M. in Wisconsin

Saying good night to the calves

8 P.M. in Mexico and Wisconsin is…

9 P.M. in Brooklyn, New York
The vroom and shush of traffic
outside the bedroom window
while Mama turns the pages
of a sleepytime tale.

Every twenty-four hours the earth rotates once on its axis. At any one of those hours, half of the earth is exposed to the sun, while the other half is in darkness. This is what we call day and night. The middle of the day, when the sun is at its height, is called noon. But when it is noon where you are, it is not yet noon to the people who live to the west of you, and it is past noon to the people who live to the east.

In 1884, to reduce confusion for travel and long-distance communication, people made an international agreement to divide the world into twenty-four time zones. Within each time zone, all clocks read the same. As you move to the west across a time zone boundary, you find that clocks are back one hour. As you move to the east, clocks are ahead one hour. There are some exceptions to this rule. For example, India's time zone is one half hour behind the time zone to the east and one half hour ahead of the time zone to the west.

NINE O'CLOCK LULLABY

Text copyright © 1991 by Marilyn Singer
Illustrations copyright © 1991 by Frané Lessac
Printed in the U.S.A. All rights reserved.
Typography by Elynn Cohen
1 2 3 4 5 6 7 8 9 10
First Edition

Library of Congress Cataloging-in-Publication Data
Singer, Marilyn.
    Nine o'clock lullaby / Marilyn Singer ; illustrated by Frané
Lessac.
        p.   cm.
    Summary: While Mama reads a sleepytime tale at 9 p.m. in Brooklyn,
people have a snack in the pantry at 2 a.m. in England, the cat
knocks over the samovar at 5 a.m. in Moscow, a family has a barbecue
at noon in Australia, and the sun is setting at 6 p.m. in Los
Angeles.
    ISBN 0-06-025647-8. — ISBN 0-06-025648-6 (lib. bdg.)
    [1. Time—Fiction. 2. Geography—Fiction.] I. Lessac, Frané,
ill. II. Title.
PZ7.S6172Ni 1991   90-32116
[E]—dc20   CIP
                                                         AC